Praise for Pat Croce and the *New York Times* bestseller, *I Feel Great and You Will Too!*

From his days as a college jock to his years studying physical therapy and his purchase of the Philadelphia 76ers, Croce has been one of those larger-than-life people who regard every obstacle as an opportunity for triumph . . . This book is as funny and energetic as its author.

—*Publishers Weekly*

Croce comes across loud and clear in his memoir-slash-motivational program.

—Brad Hooper, *Booklist*

Pat Croce's [voice] crackles with confidence . . . Through smarts and sweat, by using flash and cash, by being a wildly exuberant, over-the-top character, Croce has become the most popular person in Philadelphia.

—Stu Bykofsky, *Philadelphia Daily News*

Pat Croce is the model and mentor tion of sports and business entrep we follow.

—Ted Leonsis, president, America Online's Interactive Properties Group

A great read from a fascinating man. Pat Croce tells his life story with the humor, honesty, and good sense that has long won him so many friends and admirers—a group I am lucky and proud to belong to.
—Senator John McCain

I thoroughly enjoyed Pat Croce's book, *I Feel Great and You Will Too!* It's a fast, funny, candid, and intelligent read. It's great to read a story that reminds us that the American Dream lives on!
—Bruce Willis

Pat Croce's amazing success story is about motivation, inspiration, and a fair dose of chutzpah! Pat's advice, liberally sprinkled throughout the book, will cause you to nod in agreement—and smile.
—David Stern, NBA Commissioner

[Pat Croce's] life story is truly inspirational and I consider myself blessed to have been a small part of it. I'll never forget our friendship and what it meant to my career and life.
—Mike Schmidt, member, Baseball Hall of Fame

Pat Croce is a true inspiration to anyone who has ever had a dream.
—Brian L. Roberts, president, Comcast Corporation

For someone like me who needs an inspiring, motivating, get-my-spirits-up-out-of-my-shoes shot in the arm, Pat Croce's book comes straight from heaven! He's Saint Croce, as far as I'm concerned!

—Chuck Barris, creator of *The Dating Game, The Newlywed Game,* and *The Gong Show*

This is a foot-stomping (oops, I'd better embrace another part of his skeleton), knee-slapping good read. I don't know what Pat eats for breakfast, but I want some of what gives him that fire in da belly.

—Jimmy Buffett

Pat Croce's life is packed with amazing, humorous, and inspirational incidents. He obviously is someone who has prevailed through dedication, honest effort and a unique aptitude for dealing successfully with challenges. Croce's precepts of customer service are must reading for anyone who deals with the public.

—Joe Paterno, head coach, Penn State Football

[Croce] is smart and creative and driven. But he is also personable and funny and straightforward.

—*Intelligencer Journal* (Lancaster, PA)

I Feel Great and You Will Too! is an engaging blend of autobiography and business acumen.

—*Advance of Bucks County*

Pat may live in a swell mansion in Villanova but at heart he's still a hell-raisin', high-fivin', Harley-ridin' Delco kid—no pretensions, just a raw lust for livin'. . . . The result is a book that's pure Pat—honest, direct, funny and profane, and that brims with street smarts, home-spun wisdom, and unabashed spirit and exuberance. It's the literary equivalent of Prozac, Norman Vincent Peale with pirate tattoos.

—Art Carey, *Philadelphia Inquirer*

[Croce's] ascension to power—given where he started—will no doubt inspire unfamiliar non-Philadelphians. His life—and this is being said without irony or cynicism—is proof of what the power of positive thinking can accomplish.

—Tim Whitaker, *Philadelphia Weekly*

The best Hollywood sports story to come out of Philadelphia since *Rocky*.

—Scott Greenstein, chairman, USA Films

A FIRESIDE·BOOK

Published by Simon & Schuster

New York London Toronto Sydney Singapore

110%

110 Strategies for Feeling Great EVERY DAY

PAT CROCE

with Bill Lyon

Foreword by Lance Armstrong

FIRESIDE
Rockefeller Center
1230 Avenue of the Americas
New York, NY 10020

First Fireside Edition 2002
First published by Running Press Book Publishers, Philadelphia
and London

FIRESIDE and colophon are registered trademarks
of Simon & Schuster, Inc.

For information regarding special discounts for bulk purchases,
please contact Simon & Schuster Special Sales at
1-800-456-6798 or business@simonandschuster.com

Designed by Bonni Leon-Berman
Manufactured in the United States of America

10   9   8   7   6   5   4   3   2

Library of Congress Cataloging-in-Publication Data
   Croce, Pat.
   110% : 110 strategies for feeling great every day / by Pat Croce
with Bill Lyon ; foreword by Lance Armstrong.
      p. cm.
      1. Conduct of life—Miscellanea. I. Title: One hundred ten percent.
II. Lyon, Bill. III. Title.

   BF637.C5 C77 2002
   158.1—dc21   2002026786

   ISBN 0-7432-3514-2

To my hero,

Michael,

and my princess,

Kelly,

for making your

parents feel great

ACKNOWLEDGMENTS

I would like to thank all of those people who make me feel great through their smiles, screams, high-fives, gestures of thanks, words of encouragement, and demonstrative support at work and play.

110% would not have been possible without the support and friendship of Running Press publisher, Buz Teacher, the creative editing talents of Jennifer Worick, the able assistance of Susie Barbacane, and the wit and wisdom of my coauthor, Bill Lyon.

10%

FOREWORD

Just like Pat Croce, I'm the kind of person who can't sit still. We greet the morning with enthusiasm, excited about the opportunity to improve on the day before, and to embrace the challenges that lie ahead.

That's what life is all about: taking advantage of every minute because you don't know where the ride will take you next.

Pat Croce's strategy sounds too good to be true. Spending time with my family, heading out for a long ride on my bike, letting go of my worries . . . These are activities I enjoy every day, and they're all on his list. It's not about drastically changing your life, it's finding happiness in the little things that surround you daily, and seeking out new adventures.

Whether you're on the go or need a little push, *110%* offers quick tips to jump-start your everyday life. You can pick it up for instant inspiration, positive reinforcement, whether the odds are for or against you.

110% reveals the philosophies behind Pat Croce's revved-up assault on life. Pat is *alive,* and that attitude rubs off on anyone who comes in contact with him or who reads his books.

What are you waiting for? As Pat says, "Today is a new day; seize it."

—*Lance Armstrong*

INTRODUCTION

So, how are you?

These are the standard replies:

"Not bad."

"Okay."

"Pretty good."

"Hangin' in."

"Hangin' on."

"Fine."

Just once, try this instead: "I feel great!" Say it with gusto, with conviction, with wattage.

And then watch the other person recoil. The reaction will be somewhere between disbelief and envy.

I've been shouting "I feel great!" for so long now that people shout it to me before I can open my mouth.

And, yes, I know exactly what you're thinking: *Oh, please. It is not possible for anyone to feel great, to be in such an effervescent mood, all the time.*

Well, of course it's not.

But in the bleak moments, there are thoughts you can summon to help overcome depression, pain, sorrow, and negativity. Because for the most part, we—and not our circumstances—determine how we feel.

We all have our low-tide days. We all have our moods, low points when it is so tempting to succumb to discouragement and despair. It's in these moments of vulnerability that our thinking can become distorted.

It doesn't take much effort to think yourself into a real funk. Have you ever twisted and tossed in the sheets and let your imagination magnify whatever problems you might be having? Isn't it amazing how swiftly that mole hill can blossom into Mount Everest just by percolating in your own mental juices?

If we can create our own angst, we can also create our own happiness. There is an old saying that happiness comes from within, but sometimes we need help to coax it out.

Which is what this book is intended to do.

One hundred ten . . . well, 110 what, exactly?

Techniques? Tricks? Tactics?

Secrets? Strategies?

Yes, yes, yes.

Yes and yes.

But there are no magic potions within these pages. No instant cures. No snap-your-fingers-and-your-problems-are-gone guarantees.

You will not arise from one reading and suddenly reside in Eden or Utopia, content beyond all expectations, anxieties nowhere to be found.

But what *110%* can do is help to remove some of the psychological blocks that bedevil you daily. These are one hundred ten suggestions for elevating your mood, and I suspect that you already have a few strategies of your own to add to the list.

And if you do, then by all means share, share, share.

The ironic thing about happiness is that we make the pursuit of it harder than it has to be. We go about it backasswards. We chase after happiness when what we should be doing is eliminating unhappiness. Just let go of the negative and the depressing. People who make studies of these things report that you can access your inner happiness at will.

Any place.

Any time.

Happiness is one state of being where you are in control. You have the power to think: *Know what? I feel great!* And you have the power to give that thought voice, to say it out loud, which is the first step in convincing yourself that it is true.

Years ago I did a daily one-hour radio show in Philadelphia. It was concerned with health and fitness. I used "I feel great!" as my signature line. It caught on with the public. But it was more than a gimmick. It was my motivation.

And at every watershed moment in my life, I have found reason to shout it. Sometimes in moments of unbridled joy. Sometimes in moments of unendurable pain.

When my kids were born, I cried it.

When the deal was sealed to purchase the Philadelphia 76ers, I screamed it.

When we won the NBA draft lottery, I shrieked it.

When a paramedic leaned over me on a rain-swept stretch of highway, where my bones were scattered like pebbles, I croaked it.

When I was discharged from the hospital, and was fortunate to have avoided amputation, I whispered it.

When my first book made the *New York Times* Bestseller List, I yelped it. And every day—sometimes hundreds of times—I respond with it whenever anyone asks me how I'm doing.

It has become habit. Reflex. But it never grows old and it is always useful.

While I was in the hospital for two weeks after a horrendous motorcycle accident that almost sheared off my leg . . . while I endured the first of several surgeries . . . while my body played host to a parade of plates and rods and screws . . . I teetered on the edge of giving up.

But I thought how lucky I was that I had lived.

I thought how lucky I was to have the love and support of my family and so many friends.

I thought how lucky I was compared to the scores of people stricken with fatal diseases.

I thought that surely God had a reason for this, that there would be a way to salvage something useful from the experience.

I thought, in other words, thoughts that were positive, thoughts that could pull me back from the edge of giving up.

I told myself that I felt great—even when I didn't.

And then I began to think of the techniques I had learned that helped alter my thinking, helped adjust my attitudes, helped improve my moods . . . in short, techniques that make feeling great possible.

And here they are . . .

1 PUT IT IN PERSPECTIVE

"From the lowly perspective of a dog's eyes, everyone looks short."

—Chinese proverb

"Every moment is a golden one for him who has the vision to recognize it as such."

—Henry Miller

Think about yourself . . . right now!

You are holding this book with healthy hands. You are reading this book with perky peepers (even though, like me, you might be wearing glasses). And you are processing this book's contents with an attentive mind.

Not everybody is as fortunate as you.

When you put your everyday world in perspective (no crippling disease, blindness, or head injury for example), you realize that life is pretty good. When you put your feet in the shoes of others and then jump right back into your own, you find that you might enjoy the fit. Get used to them, and get the most out of them.

Remember all of your own yesterdays that may not have been so good as today. And, if by chance, this is your low point, buckle down and keep looking up—things could always be worse. But if you keep your life in perspective, things will only get better.

RISE AND SHINE 2

"Early to bed, early to rise, makes a man healthy, wealthy, and wise."

—Ben Franklin

"Never get up before breakfast. If you have to get up before breakfast, eat breakfast first."

—Anonymous

There are some drinking establishments that advertise what they call "The Attitude Adjustment Hour." It comes at the end of the day, when your springs are uncoiled and you are ready to bounce off the walls.

But the time to get those springs jumping is at the beginning of the day. The most important attitude adjustment occurs right on the edge of your bed in the morning, as you swing your legs onto the floor and prepare to greet the day.

How you approach your day at the very outset will pretty much dictate how your entire day will go. Attitude has a way of determining performance.

If you're excited, you can make things exciting.

3   E X E R C I S E

"Whenever you get the urge to exercise, lie down. If you're lucky, the urge will pass."

—Rodney Dangerfield

"If you don't find time to exercise you'll have to find time for illness."

—Anonymous

There is this magic drug. You don't need a prescription for it. It will elevate your mood. It is legal. It is free. It will give you the glow of well-being, and there's no hangover.

Believe it or not, such a miracle drug does exist.

It is called an endorphin. It is a chemical released by your brain while you are exercising. You have probably heard references to it under other monikers, such as a runner's high. It is not, however, necessary to run a marathon to open your endorphin spigot.

Just move. Set your body in motion. You won't believe the returns. The cool thing about energy is that the more of it you expend, the more of it you have. Oxygen cleanses your brain, clears away the cobwebs. You suddenly become alert. You think clearer. You feel confident, alive. You want to tackle your problems instead of running away from them.

So what are you waiting for? Get off the couch and get into some sneakers.

VOLUNTEER

4

"*We make a living by what we get, but we make a life by what we give.*"
—Norman MacEwan

"*I want three volunteers—you, you, and you.*"
—The Army

The good we do has a way of coming back to us. The first thing you notice when you give to others is a warm feeling that radiates quickly throughout your body. It's not unlike the effect of those endorphins discussed in the previous strategy.

You don't have to look far to find a cause. I spread some of my volunteer work among the Juvenile Diabetes Foundation; Sister Mary's Project H.O.M.E. for the building of shelters and revitalization of inner city neighborhoods; and Read for Ronald, which not only encourages literacy but supports the Ronald McDonald House that is associated with Children's Hospital of Philadelphia.

Volunteers assisted my own children in learning the basics of baseball, basketball, and soccer. Every time we thanked them, they had the same response: "*We* are the ones who benefited from the experience."

The greatest gift we can give another person is our time.

5

"Sex is the second greatest invention. I forget what was the first."

—Marilyn Monroe

"Whoever named it necking was a poor judge of anatomy."

—Groucho Marx

Sex is both a release and a restorer. It melts, relaxes, soothes.

The French like to think that if they didn't invent sex they at least perfected it, and they have this saying: *Marriages are made in heaven, but consummated on earth.*

And if sex didn't have enough to recommend it all on its own merits, consider this: Each act burns, on average, one hundred calories.

Which gives a whole new dimension to the notion of "think thin."

SET REACHABLE GOALS

6

"A goal is nothing more than a dream with a time limit."
—Joe Griffith

"Arriving at one goal is the starting point to another."
—John Dewey

Yes, your grasp should exceed your present reach. But not by such a margin that you become discouraged and give up.

Ambition is wonderful. But your goals should be attainable, so that you find working toward them a source of pleasure and not hopeless drudgery.

Remember: The best way to eat the elephant standing in your path is one bite at a time.

7 PREPARE A TO-DO LIST

"A good plan today is better than a perfect plan tomorrow."

—Patton's Law

"No amount of genius can overcome a preoccupation with detail."

—Levy's Eighth Law

There's the list with all the tasks you have set for yourself. You feel organized and in charge and you wade in and . . .

. . . here comes one of the most self-satisfying actions in the English language:

Check.

Check.

Check.

Done.

Done.

Done.

Give yourself a hug.

Just creating a to-do list gives you an enormous sense of accomplishment. Checking off tasks as you complete them . . . well, I get a shiver up and down my spine just thinking about it.

CELEBRATE
LITTLE VICTORIES 8

"A pat on the back is only a few inches from a kick in the butt."

—Anonymous

"I'd like to pause for just a moment so that we can all celebrate the wonderfulness of . . . me."

—Groucho Marx

Who can be nicer to you than you? The better you feel about yourself, the more enthusiastic you'll be.

So take a moment to indulge in some self-congratulation when you've reached a goal. And they don't all have to be life-altering milestones. Savor the little triumphs, the small achievements. Finishing your tax return on time. Losing five pounds. Teaching your child something new.

Self-praise is a nice way to remind yourself that you're making progress, inch-by-foot-by-yard-by-mile.

9 HANG OUT WITH FRIENDS

"A friend is a present you give yourself."
—Robert Louis Stevenson

"A friend is one who dances with you in the sunshine and walks with you in the shadows."
—Anonymous

The nice thing about friends is that you can keep all the old ones and still collect new ones.

The best things in life are those things that we can share with someone else. And then the best thing after that is reliving those memories with each other.

How do you tell a real friend from the pretenders? The real deal likes you for who you are, not for what you are. You know that feeling you get when you are knee-deep in a conversation with someone and you suddenly sense that you are on the same wavelength? The feeling that you can anticipate what they are going to say? The feeling that you are not alone in this world? That feeling is what it's all about.

It makes you want to go out and collect a few new friends, doesn't it?

FEEL LUCKY 10

"Luck is what happens when preparation meets opportunity."
—Elmer G. Leterman

"It's better to be lucky than good."
—Old gambler's saying

We don't always get what's coming to us. Sometimes we get what we think is coming to us.

So why not think what's coming to you is something golden? Why not think you've been showered in four-leaf clovers and horseshoes? Who's more deserving of good fortune than you?

The cynic says: *Expect the worst, and you'll rarely be disappointed.*

And I say: *Expect the best and buy a lottery ticket.*

11 EAT GOOD FOODS
(and a bad one now and then)

"Health food makes me sick."
—Calvin Trillin

"A great step toward independence is a good-humored stomach."
—Seneca

Good food does not have to be defined as healthy and nutritious vittles. Also treat yourself to foods that *taste* good to *you*.

It's important to enjoy what you're eating, whether it's carrot sticks or a chocolate eclair.

If you do nothing but deprive yourself of any treats, you'll end up depressed. Think how gray and lifeless the world would be without pie or ice cream. The occasional indulgence is good and downright necessary for your emotional well-being.

READ

"Books are the quietest and most constant of friends, the most accessible and wisest of counselors, and the most patient of teachers."
—Charles W. Eliot

"Reading is to the mind what exercise is to the body."
—Richard Steele

I'm partial to biographies. I like to read about how people have persevered and overcome. There is usually something that you can take from another person's life and incorporate into your own—not only things to do, but things *not* to do.

Reading is one of life's great pleasures. It not only opens up the whole world for you, it expands your imagination. I start the day reading the newspaper and I usually end it by reading a book or magazine in bed.

I'm a big clipper, ripper, and tearer, too. If I read something that can help me, out it comes. You never know where the next good idea is coming from. It could be on the very next page . . .

13

CREATE A MEMORY TREASURE CHEST

"I don't like nostalgia unless it's mine."
—Lou Reed

"We all have a photographic memory. Some of us just don't have film."
—Anonymous

Keepsakes will unlock it all. Photographs, of course, are prime examples of these sentimental souvenirs. But don't forget about ticket stubs, letters, cards, medals, ribbons, jewelry, newspaper clippings, and baby shoes.

Anything that triggers your memory bank and launches you on a trip down memory lane, remembering people and places and times gone by, these mementos are the fuel that will keep you going. They are invaluable, because they are artifacts of your personal history. They tell you where you came from and sometimes even act as a road sign, pointing out a direction you should take in your future.

Store them in a treasure box and take them out from time to time. Create your own personal attic.

APOLOGIZE 14

"The greatest right in the world is the right to be wrong."

—Harry Weinberger

"An apology is when the heart takes over from the mouth."

—Anonymous

Two little words: *I'm sorry.*

And their brother and sister: *Forgive me.*

Two little words that can still the shouting or defrost the silence.

If you won't let pride or ego get in the way, those two little words will make you feel even better than the one to whom you're saying them.

15

GET CHECKED OUT

"If I'd known I was going to live this long, I'd have taken better care of myself."

—Attributed to several comedians

"Good health and good sense are two great blessings."

—Latin proverb

Most of us have our cars inspected far more often than ourselves. And, really, how smart is that?

Subconsciously, we procrastinate because we like to think that no news is good news. If we don't know there's trouble, maybe it'll just go away.

Again, how smart is that?

But a regular check-up with your family physician, dentist, and ophthalmologist can give you great peace of mind.

Remember how good it felt to say: "Look, Ma, no cavities?" And if something wrong *is* detected, it can be caught early, treated, and put behind you. How's that for real peace of mind?

TELL LITTLE WHITE LIES (to yourself) 16

"By perseverance the snail reached the ark."
—Charles Haddon Spurgeon

"People need good lies. There are too many bad ones."
—Kurt Vonnegut, Jr.

There was an elderly man who continued to run in marathons despite his advanced age, and when he was asked how he could keep up such a pace, he smiled and replied, "I tell lies to my legs."

Obviously we all have times when we would rather crawl over to the side of the road and lie down rather than keep on keepin' on. That's the time to tell a selective fib or two.

Repeat them often enough and you start to believe them. "I feel great!" works wonders for me.

Terrific concept, mind over matter. If you don't mind, then it doesn't matter.

17 BUY A COMFORTABLE PAIR OF SHOES

"It isn't the mountains ahead that wear you out, it's the grain of sand in your shoe."

—Anonymous

"There's no coaxing boots and shoes to look better than they are."

—George Eliot

Sometimes, it can feel like your soul is in your sole. Then there is nothing quite as invigorating as a new pair of shoes. Sneaks or boots, loafers or sandals, flip-flops or heels, whatever you prefer.

They can put a spring in your step and a little extra pride in your stride. Each step can energize you. Freshly shod, you're ready to get back in the race.

Sometimes, what you feel in your head starts down in your toes.

WALK BAREFOOT ON THE BEACH 18

"*Get your priorities straight. No one ever said on his deathbed: 'Gee if only I'd spent more time at the office.'*"

—H. Jackson Brown, Jr.

"*Sand between the toes will help you forget the woes between your ears.*"

—A very wise grandmother

I'm a great believer in the healing powers of hydrotherapy. The beach has a way of sharpening all your senses while at the same time releasing tensions.

And there is nothing quite as humbling as walking the beach on a starry night. You breathe in, look up, and regain a sense of the size of the universe—and your modest place in it. Those things that have been eating at you, those problems that seemed so insurmountable, suddenly shrink to insignificance.

Barefoot on the beach is a great situation in which to regain proper perspective.

19 LET YOUR WORRY GO

"We don't get ulcers from what we eat, we get them from what's eating us."

—Anonymous

"Worry is interest paid on trouble before it falls due."

—W. R. Inge

Grapes that ferment become wine. Apples that ferment become cider. Cabbage that ferments becomes sauerkraut. Worry that ferments becomes an ulcer. The key, then, is not to let your worries sit there and fester and ferment.

Go on the attack. Do what you can with what you have control over, and what is not in your control is not worth worrying about.

Remember this domino philosophy: There are only two things really worth worrying about—either you're sick or you're well.

If you're sick, either you get well or you die. If you get well, there's nothing to worry about.

If you die, there are two things to worry about—either you go to heaven or to hell. If you go to heaven, there's nothing to worry about. If you go to hell, you'll be so busy partying with all your friends there will be nothing to worry about.

RIDE THE HOBBY HORSE 20

"He enjoys true leisure who has time to improve his soul's estate."

—Henry David Thoreau

"To be able to fill leisure intelligently is the last product of civilization."

—Arnold Toynbee

To each his own. If not golf, then perhaps fishing. Or collecting. Spoons or matchbooks, it doesn't matter. Or perhaps you have more crafty interests, such as quilting or cooking. Model railroading or home brewing beer. The possibilities are limitless.

It can be a hobby you began as a child and want to expand. Or it can be something new. Either way, a hobby is stimulating and energizing.

We all need a break from time to time, and a hobby is a comforting escape. It is a vacation for your mind.

21 PLAY WITH YOUR KIDS

"In every real man a child is hidden that wants to play."

—Friedrich Nietzsche

"If you want a totally honest opinion, ask a child. They haven't learned yet how to be deceitful."

—Anonymous

One of the awesome things about kids is that when you play with them, they make you feel young. It's like a free sip from the Fountain of Youth.

It's a passage, and you return in time to a place when cynicism hadn't yet replaced innocence, when you hadn't yet succumbed to skepticism, when you still had a sense of wonder about all things.

The irony is that we're always in a rush to grow up, and only after we've done that do we realize what we've left behind. Play with your kids and you can recapture some of that, if even for just a moment.

P.S. They'll think it's pretty cool, too.

IGNORE BAD MOODS 22

"*Look at the word* problem. *Now substitute the word* opportunity."
—Ann Landers

"*Pessimist: One who, when he has the choice of two evils, chooses both.*"
—Oscar Wilde

It is said that the happiest people aren't necessarily those who have everything, it's those who make the best of everything. You know the routine: If you've got yourself some lemons, make yourself some lemonade.

But there is a reason that clichés become clichés, and that is that they are true. Lethargy and frustration are inevitable. We can't completely escape them, but we can try to deal with them. Here are some ways: *Look the other person in the eye. Stop, and look up. Coo at a baby. Say thank you. Phone home.*

You may have to accept a bad mood, but you don't have to give in to it.

23 HUG THINGS (people, trees, etc.)

"There's nothing in this world that can't be made better with chocolate and a hug."

—Anonymous

"Exchange embraces with your enemy. Then check your back for knives."

—H. L. Mencken

I'm a hugger, and proud of it. If it moves, and sometimes even if it doesn't, I'm probably going to wrap both my arms around it and squeeze away.

There's something reassuring about a hug. You get one and it makes you feel liked and appreciated. It is good for your sense of self-worth.

And when you give a hug, you're giving a part of yourself. Hugs are like boomerangs. Chances are pretty good that what you are giving is going to come back to you.

THINK "KAISEN" 24
(It's Japanese)

"There's always room for improvement. It's the biggest room in the house."
—Louise Heath Leber

"Even if you're on the right track, you'll get run over if you just sit there."
—Anonymous

Self-improvement is something you sneak up on. You make progress by centimeters and inches, not by miles at a time. You make headway the same way your lawn grows grass in the summer—when no one is paying any attention.

The important thing is to keep making it. Coaches like to tell their teams that they're either getting better or they're getting worse. But there's something worse, and that's staying where you are. That's called stagnation.

The exact opposite of stagnation is *kaisen,* which is one Japanese word for an entire philosophy, one that means "continuous improvement." A little each day. Like the inchworm. Or a blade of grass.

25 STAND TALL

"Confidence is that cocky feeling you get just before you collide with reality."

—Anonymous

"Be brave. And if you are not, then pretend to be. You'll be pleasantly surprised to learn that no one can tell the difference."

—Anonymous

Head up. Shoulders back. Chest out. Try it. You can feel the confidence and self-esteem gathering in you. That's one of the wonders of an erect posture.

Another one is physically measurable—your lungs are no longer squeezed shut like an unused accordion. Now they can dilate and expand. Your breathing capacity increases, more oxygen rushes to your brain, and you think quicker, clearer.

In martial arts I was taught to imagine that a string was stapled to the crown of my head, and that string was continually being pulled toward the ceiling. In every sense, it is elevating.

GIVE COMPLIMENTS 26

"The greatest good you can do for another is not just to share your riches but to reveal to him his own."

—Benjamin Disraeli

"I can live for two months on a good compliment."

—Mark Twain

The line at the Complaint Department is always long. The line at the Compliment Counter always has room.

Everyone wants to be acknowledged. Everyone wants to be appreciated. We all know how it feels to get that phone call that makes us brace for the criticism we're sure is to come—and the feeling that you get when, instead, praise is heaped upon you. Your spirits skyrocket!

The complaint will be heard, frowningly, and usually resented. The compliment, which costs nothing, will be remembered with a smile.

27

GET A MASSAGE

"Sometimes you just rub me the wrong way. But you know, if you use oil, it really feels good."

—Bob Hope

"I don't want to say that feels good, but I'm only giving you five more hours to stop."

—Rodney Dangerfield

Nothing feels quite as relaxing as the untying of knots. Especially the ones that are lodged in your shoulders and neck and back.

A massage is a deliciously decadent indulgence, which is all the more reason you should treat yourself to one every now and then.

It is therapeutic not only physically but mentally and emotionally as well. A massage can be the great eraser that wipes out all the mistakes and frustrations that have accumulated and are being stored in your muscles. Your body will be limber, and your mind will follow.

CHEER UP
YOUR SPACE 28

"He makes his home where the living is best."
—Latin proverb

"Home is a place where you can scratch any place you itch."
—Harry Ainsley

Whatever is "your space"—that is, the place where you work—give it life. It may be an office cubicle, the kitchen, your den, or the garage, but it's the place where you work or spend much of your time. And it should feel right to you.

It should feel like a place you want to come to, not a place you *have* to come to. So put out the pictures. Fill the vases with flowers. Create a start-up screen or a screen saver for your computer that will make you smile every day.

In my office, I've got a vintage Harley-Davidson motorcycle. Whenever I look at it, I have instant memories of pleasant things. And work doesn't seem quite so much like work.

It feels a bit like home.

29   WRESTLE

"Your conscience is just about the heaviest thing you can wrestle with."

—Anonymous

"When the cat's away, the mice will play. That's why mice have all the fun."

—Anonymous

Go ahead. You can do it. You used to do it all the time when you were a kid. Remember? On the floor. On the sofa. On the bed. Wherever and whenever the mood struck you.

So go ahead, give in to the urge. It might lead to a pillow fight. It almost certainly will lead to some tickling, and how long has it been since you were a tickler or ticklee?

Like the tango, wrestling only takes two. You and your spouse. You and your child. You and your dog. Any number can join in, of course. The one guarantee is laughter. (Who doesn't love putting someone in a headlock?) That alone makes it worthwhile.

LAUGH
(especially at life)

"He who laughs, lasts."
—Wilfred Peterson

"Laughter is the sun that drives winter from the human face."
—Victor Hugo

In the movie *Oh God* George Burns plays God, and at one point says, wistfully, "Sometimes I feel like a comedian playing to an audience that's afraid to laugh."

Life is grim enough. But with a sense of humor you can not only survive, but thrive. Giggle . . . chuckle . . . guffaw . . . belly laugh . . . treat yourself to any or all of them. It's medically beneficial, and it does wonders for your outlook.

Keep things that make you giggle close at hand, be it a photograph, an e-mail, or a page-a-day calendar. If there's a word you find particularly funny or is an inside joke with a friend, tape it to your computer or phone console.

I heard a speaker once say: "Laughter is God's gift to mankind." The cynic next me said: "And mankind is proof that God has a sense of humor."

You should always be suspicious of anyone who has no wrinkles, because if you don't have wrinkles, it means you haven't laughed nearly enough. And that's a tragedy.

31 THROW A FOOD FIT

"The body is not a temple. It's an amusement park."
—Chef Norman Aubrand

"Her pancakes were good for something; they made great Frisbees."
—Redd Foxx

Back when you were in your high chair you discovered the simple joy and the insane pleasure that can be derived from the *SPLAT!* of mashed potatoes hitting the floor, or the fascinating designs that creamed corn can make while it slides down the wall.

And, really, do any of us ever outgrow our love of a pie in the face?

Yes, your mother told you it's not polite to throw your food. But secretly she knew how much fun it really is. So go ahead, give in, and give new meaning to the phrase "food that sticks to your ribs." Or take literally the notion of a "tossed salad." Don't forget about putting egg on someone's face!

The best part is, it's not possible to throw food at each other without ending up laughing.

GET STEAMED 32

"Wash your troubles down the drain . . ."
—Old advertising slogan

"Nothing beats a soak in the tub. A million rubber duckies can't be wrong."
—Daffy Duck

Ahhhhhhhh. That hot shower spray hits you there, right *there,* right along the shoulders and the back of your neck. You can feel those bands of tension loosening already, can't you? You're melting like candle wax.

And while I'm on the subject of candles . . . there is nothing like ringing your bathtub with scented candles while you dissolve in a hot bubble bath. It feels decadent, which, according to my wife, is all the more reason to indulge.

Soaking under a shower head or in the tub is just about the most convenient luxury going. It's cheap and requires no tickets, no travel, no reservations, and no standing in line. One size fits all. Or it might even fit two. (See Strategy 5, page 22.)

33 MEDITATE

"Ohmmmmmmmm is mmmmmmmho spelled backwards. That's all I know about meditation."

—Anonymous

"Empty your mind. Of course most of us are already halfway there."

—Steven Wright

Give yourself a time out. Let all of your muscles go as limp as linguini, especially the ones between your ears.

It is not necessary to assume the lotus position or to contort your body into a pretzel in order to meditate. All you need to do is let go. Let go, if just for a moment, of everything that has a grip on you. Summon up a pleasant memory. Visualize a favorite place. Close your eyes. Slow your breathing—take a big, gulping inhale, hold it for a moment, then let 'er rip with a whooshing release-the-balloon exhale.

Do not think of all that you have to do, think of all that you have already accomplished. Meditation is like the one-minute rest between rounds in boxing. Give yourself a break from the pummeling of the daily grind.

You'll be amazed how much more focused and refreshed you'll be if you make time in your schedule for doing nothing. It's absolutely as important as all those meetings and phone calls and hours on the computer.

LET THE SUNSHINE (i.e., motivation) IN 34

"Words are the most powerful drug used by mankind."

—Rudyard Kipling

" . . . and sometime when the team is up against it, Rock, ask them to win one for the Gipper."

—George Gipp to Knute Rockne

There are mountains of motivational messages available to you—tapes, CDs, books, pamphlets. Take advantage of them. Reading or listening to them is a resounding call to arms, the blaring bugle charge to send you over the top.

We are susceptible to the sway of words. They inspire and rouse, sanctify and heal, liberate and sing. Is there, for example, any single sentence more powerful, any single sentence that can send your spirits quite like "I love you?"

Winston Churchill and his grand, defiant rhetoric rallied an island nation and motivated it to resist from the rooftops to the hedgerows. Knute Rockne and generations of football coaches after him have sent teams storming onto the field fired by the flame of words.

Corny? Sure. But just look at what corn does for livestock.

35 MARK THE MIRACLES

"Rainbows, spiderwebs, sunsets . . . the world is full of wonder if only you look."

—Anonymous

"An adult laughs an average of 15 times a day. A pre-schooler laughs an average of 400 times. The moral is: Yield to the child within you."

—Anonymous

Miracles come in all shapes and sizes. They do not all have to be on a grandiose scale, like the parting of water. In fact, if you spend all your time waiting for super nova miracles, you'll overlook all the small ones that happen all around you every single day.

All that is required is awareness and appreciation, on the scale of that laughing pre-schooler. The world is every bit as fascinating now as it was when you were in kindergarten. But we get caught up in life and we no longer see the world through the eyes of the child.

Arthur Rubinstein said: "Happiness can only be felt if you don't set any conditions." If you accept the world unconditionally, you'll see small miracles by the dozen, every day.

ASK FOR HELP

"There never seems enough time to do it right. But there always seems to be enough time to do it over."

—Anonymous

"Judge a man by his questions rather than by his answers."

—Voltaire

There was a popular ballad a few years back called "You and Me Against the World." Those are truly frightening odds, aren't they? But at least they're better than "Me Against the World." The point is, we can all use help.

It's not a sign of weakness to seek assistance. Nor is there anything wrong with confessing out loud: *I don't know.* Sometimes, that is not only the right answer, it's the best answer.

You'll be pleasantly surprised to discover how eager people are to help if you ask for help. Part of it is ego, of course—we all enjoy feeling superior from time to time, we all enjoy showing off our knowledge. But do not let your own ego get in the way. There's a saying that the truly smart man is the one who realizes just how much he does not know. Be smart. Lean on others. Ask for help.

37 WATCH THE SUN COME UP . . . OR GO DOWN

"Dawn is a term for the early morning, used by people who don't have to get up."
—Oliver Herford

"It is always darkest just before the day dawneth."
—Thomas Fuller

Are you definitely not a morning person? Even so, set your alarm some night and get up before sunrise. You can always burrow back under the covers. In the meantime, you will have witnessed a small miracle (See Strategy 35, page 52).

The only splendor to equal the majestic rise of the sun is its glorious descent. The Alpha and the Omega happening every few hours. A new beginning, a fresh start. And then a slow, spectacular unwinding. Why, you could even set your watch by these marvels.

Sunrise or sunset—either or both are good for you. No matter how often you see them, you cannot help but think, *Oh, my . . . oh, my . . .*

54

MAKE FUNNY FACES AT KIDS 38

"Life is way too serious to be taken too seriously."

—Gunars Neiders

"Childhood is the wisdom of youth before it's old enough to have opinions."

—Colin Bowles

Just for a few seconds, every now and then, permit yourself to regress. Let the years and the cares slide away, and allow yourself to become, say, four years old. Or five. Or six.

And when you pull up behind a car and there are kids staring out the back window, beat them to the punch. Cock your head at a crazy angle, cross your eyes (they won't stay that way, contrary to what your mom told you), stick out your tongue, crinkle your face. It is hard to tell who will be the most surprised, the kids or the person riding with you.

But there are sure to be giggles all around, followed by peals and squeals of laughter. By the way, a study has shown that a few dozen laughs is as beneficial as a 10-minute workout on a rowing machine.

Who knew? Kids, that's who.

39 OVERTIP

"A tip is a small sum of money you give to someone because you are afraid he wouldn't like not being paid for something you haven't asked him to do."

—Ann Caesar

"I feel a very unusual sensation—if it is not indigestion, I think it must be gratitude."

—Benjamin Disraeli

Gratuity is the fancier word for tip. It comes from gratitude. You are *grateful* for the service that has been performed for you—by a waiter or waitress, doorman or valet, barber or beautician. Of course, there are times when you aren't grateful at all.

But when the service is good, or better than good, go overboard with the tip. Word will get around soon enough. They'll be fighting over you during your next visit. These are people who depend on tips for the bulk of their income.

Human nature being what it is, overtipping will make you feel, however fleetingly, like a high roller. You'll feel indulgent. And, like Disraeli, you will feel a pleasant sensation—the knowledge that you have done a good deed.

SHOUT IT OUT: OOPS! 40

"The key to happiness is accepting one unpleasant reality every day."
—Bertrand Russell

"Don't ever promote a man who hasn't made some big mistakes—you'll be promoting a man who hasn't done much."
—Herbert H. Dow

The first word you should teach a child is "Oops!" It is the best—and safest—thing to utter after an accident. After the glass is dropped, after the window is broken, after the car door is dented, after the spaghetti sauce has dribbled onto the white shirt.

You acknowledge the mistake, and at the same time you also put it in perspective. Yes, it was an error in judgment, calculation, reach, or balance. But it was just that, an *accident,* unintentional and not premeditated. It was most certainly not a violation of any of the Ten Commandments.

The only certainty about accidents is that more will happen. So do not let the old ones live on. Bellow it out— "Oops!"—and then grant absolution all around.

41 SIT . . . STAY. . . GOOD BOY

"A loaf of bread, a jug of wine, and thou. And, oh yes, my recliner, too, please."

—Anonymous

"He does not seem to me to be a free man who does not sometimes do nothing."

—Cicero

Maybe it's a rocker. Maybe it's a recliner. Maybe it's a sofa. Maybe it's an overstuffed bean bag. Maybe it's under a tree.

Or in front of a fire. Or an aisle in the movie theater. Or in the driver's seat, watching the world go by.

Wherever it is, whatever it is, we all have a favorite seat, a secret place where we can regain our bearings, think things through, give thanks, or just ponder.

Everyone needs a safe harbor, a place to hide out, regroup, catch your breath. When you are feeling overwhelmed, take to heart the advice of Fonzie and the *Happy Days* gang: Sit on it!

MAKE YOUR HEART GO THUMPA, THUMPA, THUMPA

42

"Life is meant to be lived, not merely endured."
—Theodore Roosevelt

"If you haven't broken at least one bone, then your day isn't complete."
—Stunt man's motto

Do something thrilling. Thrilling, that is, not stupid. Thrilling, not over-the-top dangerous. Something that will get your heart going like the kettle drums in an orchestra.

We should all *carpe* the *diem* every single *diem*.

Maybe you want to sky dive. Or bungee jump. Or ride a roller coaster. Or maybe something a bit more sane and sedate. You know yourself; you know what will blow out your emotional exhaust pipe, and what will leave you feeling like a participant in your own life, not just a spectator.

Life, like a certain brand of coffee, can be good to the very last drop, so squeeze every last drop out of every day.

43

PLAN A VACATION

"A vacation is what employees are given to remind them how well the business can get along without them."

—L. L. Levinson

"First rule of vacations: Take half as many clothes as you planned, and twice as much money."

—Anonymous

Often the best part of a vacation, as with a lot of things in life, is the anticipation. Also, as with a lot of things in life, your attitude will go a long way in determining how much you will enjoy it.

Planning is important, even if it is just an overnighter. I'm a hopeless list-maker, but is there anything more frustrating than arriving at your destination only to realize just how many things you have forgotten?

Make the list, go through it, and you will not have to spend seventeen dollars for a tube of toothpaste in the chichi hotel gift shop. Plus, each time you review the list, you can renew the anticipation and savor what is to come.

KEEP A DIARY 44

"Keep a diary, and one day it'll keep you."
—Mae West

"I've been in Who's Who, *and I know what's what, but there's nothing like being in somebody's diary."*
—Mae West, again

There's an old saying that you can close your eyes to reality, but not to memories. And nothing stirs memories and brings them rushing back quite like reading your own diary. It's a verbal photo album, an instant trip back in time.

But there is value in keeping a journal or diary beyond nostalgia. In writing down your feelings at the moment, you are also dealing with them. A diary is a good way to vent, to purge yourself of pent-up emotions. You can get it all down on paper and, if you so choose, move on and never look back at your writings.

Conversely, one day when you're again under the gun, you can consult your diary to remind yourself of how you coped under similar circumstances. It could serve as a guide to what you should do now. Or not do. Like history, a diary can teach.

45 TELL THE TRUTH

"The trouble with stretching the truth is that it's apt to snap back."

—Anonymous

"Always do right. This will gratify some people, and astonish the rest."

—Mark Twain

If you always tell the truth, then you don't need a good memory. Of course, none of us ever manages to tell the truth all the time. In our search to rationalize, we invent euphemisms. We call them "fibs." Or "little white lies." Or "verbal misdirections."

Sometimes we do not tell the whole truth to spare someone's feelings, or to spare ourselves. For instance, when posed with the question, "Does this dress make me look fat?," there is only one answer for a husband, be it truthful or not.

As Oscar Wilde said, "The pure and simple truth is rarely pure and never simple."

But it is the big moments when we should tell the truth. And we know instinctively, in our heart of hearts, when those moments arise. The more uncomfortable you feel, the more pressing the need for truth.

HEED THE
SWEET TOOTH 46

"Have you heard about the new Sugar Replacement Therapy? It's called chocolate."
—Victoria Wood

"Chocolate is the answer, and it doesn't really matter what the question is."
—Anonymous

A little something sweet. Mmmm. We all get that craving once in a while. Sometimes, it's as much psychological as it is physical. Which is all the more reason to give in.

Glucose gives you a jump-start, as we know, the fabled sugar rush. Yet, strangely, while sweets will ignite your adrenaline, at the same time they have a soothing effect on your mood. So use chocolate, or the sweet of your preference, as a treat, a reward.

Dorothy Parker said: "Candy is dandy, but liquor is quicker." Candy is cheaper, though. And you don't need a designated driver.

So dive into your favorite treat, be it a candy bar from the convenience store or that sinful warm chocolate truffle cake at your favorite restaurant.

47 REMEMBER: NOTHING IS FOREVER

"The only things that you can never escape are death, taxes, and those public television pledge drives."
—Anonymous

"Time is the wisest of all counselors."
—Plutarch

This, too, we are told, shall pass. And so it will. And that is the way to view pain or discomfort, as temporary and impermanent. Try to reassure yourself that the pain will go away, the discomfort will fade. Try to hang on, first for a minute, then five, then ten.

Even the longest, coldest, bleakest night eventually has to give way to a new dawn. And while it is easy to succumb to depression and melancholy, resist the urge, console yourself with the knowledge that what is bothering you now will not endure.

Tomorrow has a way of becoming the yesterday you were worrying about today.

EXPLORE
SOMEONE
ELSE'S WORLD

48

"The person who says that a thing cannot be done should not be interrupting the person who is doing it."
—Chinese proverb

"People have one thing in common: They are all different."
—Robert Zend

Have you ever stopped to think how little you really know about many of the people you are around all the time?

Like what, exactly, do your neighbors do for a living? Or what is your coworker's family like? Where did she grow up?

Knowing such things is usually a good way to understand a person. It will help you understand why they are who they are, and how and why they react and respond as they do. So it can be instructive to visit them at home, see them in their natural habitat.

I'm not suggesting that you pry or nose around. More than anything else, it can be an education. It can also make you a better friend.

Who knows? You might find several things you didn't know you had in common.

49 START A COLLECTION

"They told me it was healthy to collect things, so I decided to collect pictures of dead presidents."
—Willie Sutton, bank robber

"They told me I should take up a hobby, so I took up drinking."
—Dean Martin

Stamps or coins, Pez dispensers or dolls, teacups or plates . . . the list of collectibles is limitless and endless. Whatever thing appeals to you, collecting it can be a source of enduring pleasure.

There is the thrill and the anticipation of a new discovery, which can spice up any trip you take. You are on a continual treasure hunt. And there is the pride of ownership, when you get to show off your collection to friends.

Collections fill leisure time, broaden your interests and knowledge, perhaps introduce you to people with similar interests—and make you easier to shop for when it's your birthday.

SEARCH FOR THE SUN 50

"Thank heavens, the sun has gone in, and I don't have to go out and enjoy it."
—Logan Pearsall Smith

"It was such a lovely day I thought it would be a pity to get up."
—W. Somerset Maughan

A comedian tells of a night spent in an after-hours saloon, and as he walks out into a blinding dawn, he points at the sun and shouts, "There it is, God's flashlight!"

Hangovers aside, the sun has a magical property beyond burning us or tanning us or making us squint.

Sunlight is uplifting.

It is a spirit-raiser. It is what makes all things grow and thrive, especially our attitude and outlook.

Denied sunlight long enough, even the cheeriest people become depressed and melancholy. So take advantage of every time the sun is out and go soak it up. The world will look brighter, in more ways than one.

51 BRING ORDER TO YOUR JUNK DRAWER

"Junk is something you throw away just before you need it."

—Anonymous

"Since we cannot hope for order let us withdraw with style from the chaos."

—Tom Stoppard

You tug and you pull and, finally, grudgingly, very grudgingly, it creaks open and reveals itself in all of its tangled splendor.

Your junk drawer.

The place where the flotsam and jetsam of your life have gone to hibernate. And, you suspect, reproduce.

It has all clumped together in one large, defiant mass. So here, then, is the chance to cater to the neat-freak in you. Believe me, it's there, even if it's buried under the clutter of your life. This is your chance to bring order out of chaos.

This can all be very symbolic—your junk drawer brought under control today can be your life being brought under control tomorrow. When it's done, ah, you will feel so proud, so utterly organized, so very much in charge.

Hey, a little self-deception can be therapeutic.

WHIP UP A SPECIAL DESSERT

52

"Kids always want to eat dessert first. Kids can be very smart, sometimes."
—Anonymous

"Life is short. Eat pie first."
—Anonymous

Gooey is always good. Maybe your taste runs to the dark side—fudge and assorted death-by-chocolate concoctions. Or perhaps you prefer a banana split? Cherry pie? Six-layer cake?

Or possibly you have your own secret weapon, some ten-kilo diet saboteur that you have perfected over the years. Well then, have it, no matter what it is (in moderation, of course). First, you'll satisfy that creative urge that lurks within us all. Second, making something special for friends or loved ones is always good for a glow. Praise is a terrific by-product.

Oh, they'll protest: *You shouldn't have.* Translation: *Are there seconds?*

53 HELP THE NEEDY

"A man's real worth is determined by what he does when he has nothing to do."

—Megiddo Message

"Charity is a thing that begins at home, and usually stays there."

—Elbert Hubbard

There are the homeless and the helpless, the abused and the abandoned. There are the blind to be read to, the elderly to be visited. There are hospitals and nursing homes crying out for volunteers.

There are school crossings to be patrolled and meals on wheels to be delivered. There are the uneducated to be taught and strays to be rescued and shivering souls who would give anything for the discarded clothing that clutters the back of your closet.

You have time on your hands? Bored? Give of yourself. Where? Just look around.

SING IN THE CAR

54

"Opera is when a guy gets stabbed in the back and instead of bleeding he sings."
—Ed Gardner

"In church they told me, make a joyful noise unto the Lord. So I sang. Don't know if it was joyful or not, but it sure was noise."
—Anonymous

Go ahead, belt it out! Turn the volume up—on the car radio and on yourself. You can do it a cappella or as a sing-along. It doesn't matter. And it doesn't matter if you know all the lyrics. And it doesn't matter if you can't carry a tune in a bucket.

Because the whole point in this is, *release*. Whether it's joy or melancholy, frustration or love, whether you're so happy you can't stand it or so sad you've got a bad case of the blues or so peeved you have to sound your barbaric yawp, let it out. You'll feel better, guaranteed.

Singing is a thing you can do so loud you shatter glass, or so soft that the melody exists only in your mind. It's a gift. Your lungs will thank you. Other body parts will be appreciative, too.

55

SURPRISE
SOMEONE

"If at first you succeed, try to conceal your surprise."

—Anonymous

Q: "So what's in the chef's surprise?"
A: "That's the surprise."

—Old vaudeville routine

Most people like surprises. Only those of the pleasant variety, of course. Anything involving balloons and ribbons and food and drink and gifts and family and friends and lots of people saying lots of nice things about you qualifies as a pleasant surprise.

The main reason we like to be surprised is that it means someone, or several someones, cares about us and cares for us. That someone cares enough to have gone to the trouble, to have spent time and energy, to plan the surprise and carry it out.

When you surprise people, you make them feel better, especially about themselves. Could there be a better reason for a surprise?

SOOTHE THE SAVAGE BEAST

"A real music lover is a man who, on hearing a soprano in the bathroom, puts his ear to the keyhole."

—Kalends

"I only know two tunes. One of them is 'Yankee Doodle' and the other isn't."

—Ulysses S. Grant

Can you hear "Battle Hymn of the Republic" and not be stirred? No way. Can you hear "When the Saints Go Marching In" and keep your feet absolutely still? Nope. Can you hear "Danny Boy" and not mist up? Not likely. Can you hear "White Christmas" and not feel nostalgic? Hardly.

Few things in life affect us quite as powerfully as music. It is the great mood adjuster. We don't know why, exactly, but music can elevate and enthrall and inspire, and just as quickly calm and soothe. Why? Well, as the late Louis Armstrong said in reply to the question, What is jazz?: "Man, if you have to ask, you'll never know."

So whether it's a Sousa march you prefer, the lonesome saxophone wail of the blues, a violin high and pure, or an acoustic guitar's throbbing whumpa-whumpa-whumpa, treat yourself to your favorite music. The cool thing about music is, it can be anything you want.

57 BANISH BOREDOM

"Happiness is often the result of being too busy to be miserable."
—Anonymous

"Somebody's boring me . . . I think it's me."
—Dylan Thomas

Boredom is like a spider's web. It ensnares you in silken, seemingly harmless bonds and pretty soon you do not even bother to resist. So it's important to give yourself a check-up from the neck up from time to time: Have I surrendered? Have I given in to the same-old, same-old?

Keep your sense of curiosity. Stay inquisitive. Stay open to new ideas, new hobbies, new books, new thoughts, new debate, new friends, new enemies, new places. Above all, stay open to learning. The end of school should be the beginning of your education.

If you can stay young in mind, you can stay young at heart. There is nothing quite as invigorating as the challenge of learning something new.

LET YOUR MIND WANDER 58

"Imagination is more important than knowledge."
—Albert Einstein

"A daydream is a meal at which images are eaten."
—W.H. Auden

Hit the off button. Now. Go ahead and let your mind wander. Remember when you were in school? It would be a hot day in spring and you were cooped up inside, chained to a desk, and you couldn't help yourself. You'd . . . begin . . . to . . . drift . . .

Well, you had the right idea and didn't know it. Daydreaming can be therapeutic and cleansing. It can also be a source of stimulation and inspiration. Some of the best concepts and creations have sprung from those moments when the brain was in neutral and allowed to find its own way in its own good time.

So set aside some fantasy time. And don't stint and don't feel guilty about it. The worst that happens is that you feel revitalized.

59 EAT A CHEESESTEAK
(or anything else greasy)

"It's not really good unless it's not really good for you."

—Anonymous

"One cannot think well, love well, sleep well, if one has not dined well."

—Virginia Woolf

Sometimes the soul must be fed, as well as the body. Sometimes you need to nourish both the psyche and the stomach. Sometimes nothing will do except shreds of meat fried to a hissing sizzle in 40-weight oil, smeared with melted cheese, slathered with onions razored thin and bubbling in grease, and then shoveled into a long roll. Remember, I'm from Philadelphia.

This is then to be consumed in large, starving-lion bites, the juices dribbling down your chin and requiring a wad of paper napkins, which will certainly—if used properly—end up in a crumpled trash heap on the side of your plate.

This is not a time for daintiness. Or apology. Or guilt.

WATCH A GOOD MOVIE 60

"Movies should have a beginning, a middle and an end. But not necessarily in that order."
—Jean-Luc Godard

"Movies are like life, only better, because you can get up and walk out any time you feel like it."
—Anonymous

Motion Pictures. Films. Flicks. Movies. They're the ultimate in escapism. You can lose yourself in them. You can guess along with the plot. You can identify with the hero or heroine.

You can recite unforgettable dialogue: "Frankly my dear, I don't give a damn." Or, "I don't think we're in Kansas any more, Toto." Or, "Louie, this could be the beginning of a beautiful friendship." Or, "Show me the money!"

Not only can you walk out of a movie if it distresses you, you can play it over and over if it pleases you, which is clearly one more advantage over reality (unless your life resembles *Groundhog Day*).

Best of all, there are so many movies lining the walls and shelves of your favorite rental joint that you can pick one to match the mood you're in.

Or how about this? Pick one to change the mood you're in.

61 SMUDGE THE GRUDGE

"The heaviest thing you can carry through this life is a grudge."

—Anonymous

"If you can't say anything good about someone, sit right here by me."

—Alice Roosevelt Longworth

Feuds and grudges, envies and resentments, jealousies and quarrels all have the same thing in common, and that is they leave you hollow and burnt out inside. They are destructive emotions because they require so much energy.

Carrying around a grudge is like carrying around a fifteen-pound weight all day long. It plumb wears you out. To carry a grudge is to invite depression. And guilt and shame are sure to follow, because you know you *should* be able to rise above pettiness. In the end, it never turns out to be worth it.

When in doubt, ask yourself: *Do I have better things to spend my passion on?* As the title of a recent bestselling book proclaims, "Don't sweat the small stuff."

And looking at the entire journey, a grudge is a roadbump on the highway of life. Pretty insignificant, don't you think?

THANK YOU
(Go ahead, say it)

62

"Gratitude is not only the greatest of virtues, but the parent of all others."

—Cicero

"Gratitude is the most exquisite form of courtesy."

—Jacques Maritain

It's common courtesy, of course, but it's so much more than that. Saying "thank you," or—even more revealing—*not* saying "thank you," shows not only your attitude but also your basic persona.

And if those two tiny words reveal sincerity, sensitivity, awareness, manners, and an overall approach to life, think what the failure to use them says about you.

Like most things that are meaningful, part of the beauty of "thank you" is its simplicity. You're giving a part of yourself and it costs nothing. You'll feel so good about yourself that you'll have more bounce to the ounce.

(By the way, thank *you* for reading my book.)

63 SHUN THE GREEN-EYED MONSTER

"Envy is the mud that failure throws at success."
—Anonymous

"Living well is the best revenge."
—George Herbert

Jealousy is one of those energy destroyers. It will sneak up on you. And then in those moments when you've succumbed to depression, when you've taken to feeling sorry for yourself, it'll bite you right in the, um, gluteus maximus.

Of course it's not possible to be human and not feel pangs of jealousy. In such moments, the trick is to counter that feeling by tallying up your own blessings. What do you have that others might envy? Health? Family? Talent? A fulfilling job? Respect? Peace of mind?

How about those everyday, but no less important, gifts? An "A" on your child's report card? Making it through a spinning class or your evening run? A successful presentation at work?

The list will grow, and surprise you. By the time you finish it, what began as something self-destructive will have turned into an appreciation of your bounty of blessings.

LOOK FOR REASONS TO CLAP

"If at first you don't succeed, try, try again. Then quit. No use being a damn fool about it."
—W. C. Fields

"Is there anything quite as annoying as a good example?"
—Anonymous

There is always something to be gained from watching a victorious moment, a winning achievement. It gives you both an appreciation and inspiration of what can be accomplished by the human spirit.

Rather than envy a success, allow yourself to be swept up in it. Go ahead and exult when someone drains the winning basket, sinks the crucial putt. It's okay to cry when your sports hero shatters an unbreakable record.

Stand and cheer at a show or a recital or a child's soccer game. Congratulate a coworker on a huge coup. Look for occasions to put your hands together and create that universal sound of approval and admiration.

When you allow yourself to feel great because someone else has succeeded, you end up feeling better about yourself. You feel that much better about your own odds against the world.

65 TURN YOUR FROWN UPSIDE DOWN

"Your attitude, not your aptitude, will determine your altitude."

—Zig Ziglar

"No great man ever complains of want of opportunity."

—Ralph Waldo Emerson

There's an old adage that every time a problem has got you down, substitute the word "opportunity" for the word "problem."

Even in ashes there is opportunity. To wit: Fire destroyed Thomas Edison's factory in 1914, and insurance was not nearly sufficient. Walking through the ruins, Edison said to his young son, Charles: "There is great value in disaster. All our mistakes have been burned up. Thank God, we can start anew."

Three weeks later, Edison unveiled the phonograph. 'Nuff said.

OWN UP TO THE BOO-BOO 66

"It's only those who never do anything who never make mistakes."
—A. Fauve

"The greatest mistake you can make in life is to be continually fearing you will make one."
—Elbert Hubbard

We're never wrong more frequently than every day. The only sure way to avoid making a mistake is to stay in bed—and of course there is always the danger that you might fall out anyway. So the best way to deal with a blunder is to admit it.

Yes, it involves the swallowing of some pride—and ego—and public face. But you'd be surprised how easily that will all go down after the first time. After a while, you won't even get indigestion.

Admitting a mistake is the first step toward correcting it. And avoiding another.

67 UNDRESS CRITICS

"A critic is a legless man who teaches running."
—Channing Pollack

"Critics are like eunuchs in a harem: They know how it's done, they've seen it done every day, but they're unable to do it themselves."
—Brendan Behan

It's an old trick given as advice to nervous people about to make a speech: Imagine your audience naked. Do the same thing with your critics.

There's always someone only too eager to find fault with whatever you're presenting as a plan or project or campaign. Your natural response is anger and resentment. You want to lash out at them in return. But that is a waste of all your precious resources.

Instead, picture them without clothes.

Or, here is one other comforting image for you: Picture your critic as Wile E. Coyote falling off a cliff with an anvil following close behind.

THE ANSWER IS "GREAT!" 68
(You were expecting something else?)

"Nothing is so contagious as enthusiasm."
—Samuel Taylor Coleridge

"Even if you're not feeling great, think how unhappy you can make your enemies if they think you are."
—Anonymous

We go through the day head down, mumbling automatically, "How are you?" In fact, we usually don't care and don't even listen to the answer. Which is all the more reason—the next time someone asks *you*—for you to bellow back: "GREAT!"

Make it a sonic boom and make it genuine, and then watch them jump. Guaranteed, it will bring them to a stop, and their eyes will widen. You can hear the wheels turning: *Really? Great?*

Say it often enough and you'll start to convince yourself. Soon, they'll be smiling when they ask you, because they know what's coming. Who knows, they themselves might even decide to try it on for size.

69 PAT A PET

"Let me be the kind of person my dog thinks I am."

—A prayer

"The best thing about pets is, they're the only creatures who will accept you just the way you are."

—Anonymous

Most of them spend their days waiting—for you. So each time you pass them, give 'em a pat or a pet, or several. Hugs and cuddles are good, too. You'll never see greater gratitude.

It is good for your health, too. Medical studies show that stroking dogs or cats lowers blood pressure, and brings a sense of tranquility and peace. When you are listening to a contented purr or a gentle panting, it's hard to remember what got you so angry and worked up in the first place.

Pets understand the value of just sitting, or in lying down. They were enjoying the benefits of a Zen philosophy far before it became popular. Join them in their stillness from time to time. You'll both benefit.

SURPRISE A STRANGER . . . SAY HELLO

70

"If you judge people, you have no time to love them."
—Mother Teresa

"I have always depended on the kindness of strangers."
—Tennessee Williams

You're walking toward each other. Or you're in an elevator. You develop a sudden burning interest in your shoes. The stranger begins to look at the sky or the roof as though he's never seen either one before.

It will continue like that, guards up, defense mechanisms activated, unless you make the first move. So go ahead. Risk it. To a person you have never seen before in your life—and likely may never again—offer a greeting.

It is worth it just for the look of astonishment. It's also worth it for the feeling that will come over you. "Hello" is an affirmation that we are all in this same leaky boat together, and in the end all that we have is each other.

71 POWER OFF
(Nap, that is)

"On your list of things to do, always get your nap out of the way first."

—Anonymous

"As far back as kindergarten we learn that naps are good for you. Then 40 years go by and we rediscover that wisdom."

—Anonymous

Every engine needs a pit stop now and then. Even yours. So come in out of the rat race, where everyone is tailgating everyone else, bumping and jockeying for position, and give yourself a chance to rev up.

We're told early on about the importance of getting eight hours of sleep every night. That's not always possible. But a nap can be the great eraser of that mistake. Ten minutes or half an hour, it doesn't take long for a recharge.

You know how you'll nod off and awake with a start? You think you've slept for hours, only to look at the clock and discover that it has been just seventeen minutes? That's nature's way of telling you that these little breaks are more refreshing than you realize.

Help yourself to seconds.

SAY A LITTLE PRAYER (or several)

"Work as if it all depends on you. Pray as if it all depends on God."

—My Mom

"Properly understood and applied, [prayer] is the most potent instrument of action."

—Mohandas K. Gandhi

A group of parishioners is asked by the pastor if they all pray regularly to God, and if so, what do they pray for?

One replies, for health.

Another, for happiness.

Another, for a better-paying job.

And another, for salvation.

One woman shakes her head at each answer and when it is her turn says: "I believe in God and I pray He believes in me."

Does prayer really help? It's like chicken soup—it can't hurt.

73 ENJOY THE NOW

"Procrastination is the thief of time."
—Edward Young

"One today is worth two tomorrows."
—Benjamin Franklin

In the smash musical *Annie,* the show-stopping song tells us: "Tomorrow, tomorrow . . . you're only a day away." And while the sentiment is nice enough—that there is always the promise of another dawn—you should not dwell on tomorrow.

Mainly because you'll miss the present, which was tomorrow only yesterday after all, and which can be pretty swell on its own. Think about the Latin term *carpe diem*—you ought to seize today and then squeeze it dry.

And here is one other really good reason to live in the moment: Tomorrow, as you may have heard, is promised to no one.

RESOLVE TO BE HAPPY

74

"Most folks are about as happy as they make up their minds to be."

—Abraham Lincoln

"Happy is when you have a scratch for every itch."

—Ogden Nash

The Bobby McFerrin smash song has it right: Don't worry. Be happy. Of course, it's not possible to do either, or both, of those things continually. Life keeps getting in the way.

But happiness, like so many things, begins with a frame of mind. You can think yourself, sometimes *will* yourself, into a mood. Happy is preferable. You get more done. You feel better. People feel better about you.

We can't always control what happens to us, but we can control how we react to it, how we let it affect us. Hopefully, we do that happily.

75 SMILE!

"You're never fully dressed until you wear a smile."

—Charley Willey

"She gave me a smile I could feel in my hip pocket."

—Raymond Chandler

You can choose to wear a scowl or a smile.

The smile uses less energy and fewer muscles, and is heartily recommended. The smile is contagious. The smile will get you smiles back.

The scowl is off-putting. The scowl will get you . . . well, you'll notice people cross the street when they see you coming.

Of all the things you put on, no matter how spiffy or polished or buffed or pressed they may be, none is more important, none will make a more lasting impression, than a smile.

A simple turning up of the corners of the mouth can do wonders for how you feel, and how others feel about you.

DO YOUR BEST 76

"The excellent is new forever."
—Ralph Waldo Emerson

"Excellence in any art or profession is attained only by hard and persistent work."
—Theodore Martin

You know that old saying, about how it only costs a little more to go first class? Well, the same philosophy applies to your efforts in any endeavor. You have something to do, so why not do it the best you can?

Or, to be more blunt, take your best shot. A number of things are apt to follow, all of them good.

You are less likely to make mistakes.

You will soon build a reputation as someone reliable and conscientious.

Pride in your effort will enhance your self-esteem.

Soon, your best becomes more than a sometime thing. It becomes a habit.

77 PERFORM RANDOM ACTS OF KINDNESS

"One can always be kind to people about whom one cares nothing."
—Oscar Wilde

"No good deed goes unpunished."
—Clare Booth Luce

This is your chance to play guardian angel or the invisible genie. You do a favor for the sheer pleasure of it, for the warm glow that will radiate through you afterwards. You do it anonymously. You don't do it for the attention or the praise or the gratitude. You do it for a stranger, for someone you've never met and probably will never see again.

Stick some quarters in a parking meter that's expired. Shovel the snow in the driveway of a neighbor whom you've never met. Buy a ticket to the movies for someone behind you in line. The opportunities are all around you. You are going to be amazed at how good you are going to feel.

Oh, and if caught, simply tell them, "Pass it on."

GOSSIP
(only about the
good stuff)

"I hate to spread rumors, but what else can one do with them?"

—Amanda Lear

"Of every ten persons who talk about you, nine will say something bad, and the tenth will say something good in a bad way."

—Antoine Rivarol

It doesn't always have to be dirt that we wallow in and then track around. Gossip tends to be petty and mean-spirited and small-minded. Guess what? It doesn't have to be that way.

You can help reverse it. Instead of spreading and embellishing the word about someone's misfortune and misdeeds, try trumpeting triumphs and successes. Substitute backslapping for backbiting. Say it to someone's face, not behind his or her back.

You'll become trusted, a person others are eager to share their secrets with, and you will become known as someone who gave gossip a good name.

79 FLOWER POWER

"What really flatters a person is that you think them worth flattering."
—George Bernard Shaw

"Every flower is a soul blossoming in Nature."
—Gérard de Nerval

Flowers are the ultimate flattery. It's a hard, hard heart that isn't melted by the arrival of a bouquet or a floral arrangement. (Or a gift basket of some sort; it is, after all, the thought that counts.)

It is as though you have given someone a sunrise all over again. The smells, the colors of fresh flowers, are intoxicating. They bring the outside inside, and give a room a feeling of serenity or vibrancy.

They are usually unexpected, which only adds to their impact. The thoughtfulness they suggest lasts long after they do.

DO IT BY MAIL 80

"An announcement guaranteed to cheer the loneliest of hearts: 'You've got mail!'"
—Anonymous

*"Sir, more than kisses, letters mingle souls /
For, thus friends absent speak."*
—John Donne

It can be e-mail or it can be snail mail. My personal preference is for the old-fashioned handwritten letter because it requires more effort and that alone enhances its value and attests to its sincerity.

But either way, by computer or postage, a note or letter that acknowledges a success, sympathizes with a difficulty, or simply hopes that all is well with you and yours, is an automatic day-brightener.

That you took the time to write speaks volumes. Literally.

81 PLANT A SEED

"A garden is a thing of beauty and a job forever."
—Anonymous

"What a man needs in gardening is a cast-iron back, with a hinge in it."
—Charles Dudley Warner

It is such a symbolic act. Drop a seed into a hole and watch it grow. It's a triumph of hope and persistence over all the odds. And there's something both stirring and soothing about plunging your hands into soil. It's a primal pleasure. Maybe it feels satisfying because we are all linked to the good earth.

You don't have to maintain a full-fledged garden. It can be a small patch of sod. It can even be in the form of a window box or two if you're pressed for space. Maybe you are growing some tomatoes, red as rubies and bursting with juices. Maybe corn, if you've got room. Herbs, if you don't.

The crop itself isn't important. It's the act of growing that matters, from seed to harvest. It is tangible reaffirmation for you, every day, of the miracle of life. You'll take fewer things for granted and you'll have something delicious to eat.

GO AHEAD, ASK FOR THE IMPOSSIBLE

82

"Possibly means no, in three syllables."

—L. L. Levinson

"If men cease to believe that they will one day become gods then they will surely become worms."

—Henry Miller

If you never ask, then the answer is always "no."

But if you keep asking, then maybe one day the answer will be "yes." You'll never know, though, if you don't keep asking. Ask, pray, plead, pursue.

And then repeat the process.

It doesn't cost any more to ask for the impossible than it does to ask for the easily attainable. Besides, how do you know, for absolute certain, if a thing really *is* impossible? All it means is that it hasn't been done yet.

You can be the first.

83 SING THE BLUES

"Sympathy is what one person offers another in exchange for the details."

—Anonymous

"'Tis the only comfort of the miserable to have partners in their woes."

—Miguel de Cervantes

An ear to bend. A shoulder to cry on. A cold one in the hand and the blues in both ears, and most important, someone who'll listen without interrupting and then nod in all the right places.

It can do wonders for the soul, this time-honored process of unburdening yourself to a empathetic audience. Yes, wallowing in your misery is an act of self-indulgence, but we all have our moments of despair, and the best way out is to not hold it in. Sometimes you need to hit rock bottom before you can push yourself back up to the surface. And sometimes you need to share your pain.

Talking is therapeutic.

You vent.

You purge.

Cry if you like.

 Sing the blues until the cows come home or the dogs start wailing, whichever comes first. Go ahead. You're allowed.

DRESS TO REST

"Pardon me while I slip into something more comfortable."
—Several Hollywood sex sirens

"It is an interesting question how far men would retain their relative rank if they were divested of their clothes."
—Henry David Thoreau

Lounge clothing can run the gamut. There are no rules. It's whatever works for you. Perhaps your favorite outfit is a satin robe and elegant slippers. Or flannel pajamas might be more to your liking. Maybe you change into baggy sweats, two times too large, as soon as you get home.

The style is not what is important, but how the clothes make you feel. We all have our favorite duds in which to vegetate and chill out. They're the clothes that . . . well, just the thought of putting them on is enough to make you feel relaxed.

So, from time to time, treat yourself to an article or two of clothing that, when on, whispers suggestively to you, "We've got nothing to do and we're gonna do it really well. . . ."

85 SAY NO-NO TO TICK-TOCK

"Time is a storm in which we are all lost."
—William Carlos Williams

"The best way to fill time is to waste it."
—Marguerite Duras

It's easy to become a prisoner of time. Easier, still, to become a slave to it.

And that tiny mechanism that straps onto your wrist or hangs from a pendant or is on a fob and chain has a way of ruling your life. So at those times when time is not important, when there is no need for urgency or punctuality, when time really doesn't matter, then strip yourself.

Rid yourself of every timepiece, if only temporarily.

You're free!

And during idle moments, try to solve this conundrum: How is it that time flies and yet also stands still?

DECLARE A HOLIDAY

86

"No man needs a vacation so much as the man who has just had one."
—Elbert Hubbard

"Cultivated leisure is the aim of man."
—Oscar Wilde

Instead of a gift wrapped and tied with a bow, give a *day* to a special someone. The itinerary is up to them. You are along to make sure their wishes are fulfilled.

"It's your holiday," you tell them. "Whatever you want to do, to see, to eat, to drink—that is exactly what we shall do." The only rules are that no interruptions are allowed, especially from work, and everyone has to have a good time.

An amusement park, a baseball game, a day at home watching movies and eating ice cream. Your holiday can be as ambitious or as lazy as you desire. The idea is to escape from the norm.

The nice thing about making your own holiday is that you do not have to wait for it to come around on any calendar.

It is not subject to seasons, only to your whims.

87 MAKE PEACE

"May God defend me from my friends; I can defend myself from my enemies."
—Voltaire

"A friend in need is a . . . pest."
—Anonymous

The peace we speak of here is peace of mind, and it is one of the nobler, more worthwhile things you can help someone else achieve. And it doesn't take much, just a genuine concern for others.

All that is required is a phone call or a visit to offer compassion and concern to someone who is struggling.

With alcohol, perhaps. Or family. Food. Finances.

With all of the worries that besiege us daily, none of us is immune.

The peace you help make possible now within another will be returned to you sometime down the road in the karmic future.

MAKE IT A NIGHT (in school)

"I read Shakespeare and the Bible and I can shoot dice. That's what I call a liberal education."

—Tallulah Bankhead

"Stand firm in your refusal to remain conscious during algebra. In real life, I assure you, there is no such thing as algebra."

—Fran Lebowitz

You are never too young to learn, and never too old. So, go ahead, enroll in night school. Take a class. Stir the gray matter. Recharge your brain cells. Challenge yourself. You'll find it invigorating.

You don't need to study Shakespeare, although there's certainly nothing wrong with that.

Maybe you'd like to learn tai chi. Brush up on your high school French. Learn photography.

How about carpentry? Poetry? Pottery? Cooking? Dancing?

The possibilities are limitless. So are you, if you set your mind to it.

89 PICTURE THIS

"*Sometimes you can tell a large story with a tiny subject.*"
—Eliot Porter

"*I hardly recognize myself in this picture. For which I shall be eternally grateful.*"
—Katharine Hepburn

We all try to remember. We have good intentions. But we forget. And in so doing, we allow memories to slip away without getting them on the record.

Don't wait for a vacation to get out your camera. You don't need to reserve your picture-taking for faraway places. You don't have to wait until Christmas. Snap away now. In your own yard, your own house.

All your friends . . . how many pictures do you have of them? And your family? It's easy enough to remedy. Aim and click. Point and shoot. Capture the silly, the serious, and your everyday experiences. Then it is forever, even if times change. How old *is* that roll of film in your camera? What's even on that film? Finish the roll and find out.

MOVE YOUR FEET TO THE BEAT

90

"I wish I could shimmy like my sister Kate. She shivers like the jelly on a plate."

—Armand J. Piron

"Dancing is a perpendicular expression of a horizontal desire."

—George Bernard Shaw

Whatever the rhythm you hear in your heart, give in and dance to it. Dance in joy and celebration. Boogie away the blues. Waltz to a moment of triumph. Rock out to work out the frustration.

Sway and stomp, guide and slide. Barefoot or in heels, give yourself over to the music.

Dancing is poetry of the feet. You can do it with a partner. You can do it solo. You can pretend to be Fred Astaire and/or Ginger Rogers. Or Gene Kelly, just singin' and dancin' in the rain.

You can have two left feet; it doesn't matter. Just surrender to the moment.

91 MIRROR, MIRROR . . .

"The mirror shows not only who you are, but where you are in life—and what it took to get there."

—Anonymous

"All mirrors are magical mirrors; never can we see our faces in them."

—Logan Pearsall Smith

Check for wrinkles. Got 'em? Because if you don't have any crow's feet or creases, remember what we told you: You haven't laughed nearly enough (See Strategy 30, page 47). So fret not.

Wrinkles and crinkles, furrows and creases . . . all they are, those lines, are highways mapping out your journey through life.

So now that you're done with the self-examination, look into the mirror and again do a careful assessment. Don't be so hard on yourself this time. Search for the good qualities and important experiences that those lines signify. The joyful moments, the hard-won victories.

Hmmmm. Not bad. Not bad at all. All things considered, not too shabby.

Oh, and here's the best possible use of all for a mirror: to rehearse your smile.

PRACTICE
GAMESMANSHIP 92

"Three shouts that you should never, ever outgrow: 'You're it!' 'King me!' 'Go fish!'"
—Anonymous

"If you watch a game, it's fun. If you play it, it's recreation. If you work at it, it's golf."
—Bob Hope

Played any games lately? Yahtzee? Checkers? Chess? Tag? Hide-n-Seek? Charades? Bridge? Pinochle? Scrabble?

Clue? Parcheesi? Trivial Pursuit? Canasta?

It has been awhile, hasn't it? Didn't used to be that way, though, did it? When you were a kid, didn't it seem like you were always playing something? Well, you shouldn't completely lose that kid just because you're adult now. A game is still a nice break. And it's liable to awaken old memories, when things weren't nearly so complicated.

No playmates? There's always solitaire. But the same rules still apply: No peeking!

93 LOOK FOR THE LIGHT

"Sometimes it turns out that the light at the end of the tunnel is from an oncoming train."

—Anonymous

"Every thing that is done in the world is done by hope."

—Martin Luther

Somewhere, it's out there. The happy ending. The resolution to a problem eating you alive. The answer that always seems just beyond your grasp. It's out there, really it is, that fabled light at the end of the tunnel.

In moments of dark doubt, try to recall other occasions of despair, times when you were certain that the fix you were in was permanent. Yet it wasn't. Things have a way of working out. Perhaps the most soothing Biblical passage of all is "This, too, shall pass."

Have faith. Give yourself over to the master plan. Faith has been described, in high jump terms, as nothing more than throwing your heart over the bar—and letting your body follow.

BE A NATURE WATCHER 94

"*I am the sort who would never notice a bird building a nest unless it came and built it in my hat in the hat room of the club.*"

—Stephen Leacock

"*A fisherman is someone who sits around on river banks doing nothing because his wife won't let him sit around doing nothing at home.*"

—*The Irish News*

You don't have to go on a safari. Traversing the Appalachian Trail isn't necessary. The wonders of nature surround us on a daily basis. But we tend either to take them for granted or pay them no mind.

That's a mistake. There's much to learn from and admire in nature.

For example, watch the ant at work. He is incredibly industrious and can tote many times his own weight. Or for real gossamer beauty and intricate engineering, check out spider webbing glistening with morning dew. You could buy or build a bird bath or a bird feeder. Or invest in a modest aquarium.

Nature is good for your perspective. It gives you a whole new appreciation of life and your place in the world.

95

BE A WELCOME WAGON

"A neighbor is that person we always meant to visit."

—Anonymous

"Love your neighbour, yet pull not down your hedge."

—English proverb

What do you know about your neighbors? What do they know about you? Maybe they live right next door. Or the next floor up, or one flight below. In many instances, the distance might as well be a trip to the moon and back for as much as you visit them.

We have good intentions about saying hello, but we never seem to get beyond the quick wave or the cursory nod. If they are lucky, they might get both in passing.

Close the distance. Go on over and knock on their door. Come bearing gifts. Simple offerings will do: a favorite recipe, your killer dessert, some ice cream, or a six-pack. It's your presence that speaks volumes.

And you might have just initiated a beautiful friendship.

MUTE THE DAY

"Noise is a stench in the ear."
—Ambrose Bierce

"Silence is the element in which great things fashion themselves."
—Maurice Maeterlinck

Look on your remote control. There's a little button there that can do magic: MUTE.

Press it.

Ahhhh. The sweet sound of silence.

You can do that to your day, not just your TV. Wrap yourself in a cocoon of quiet. Turn off the cell phone. Turn off the pagers and the beepers. The phone is verboten. E-mail is outlawed. Make yourself unreachable, if only for a few delicious, mysterious moments.

You are free to do anything you want. Considering that no one can now find you, just luxuriating in that thought may be all you need.

97

TAKE A DAY TRIP

"I do not like work even when someone else does it."

—Mark Twain

"You're never too old to enjoy playing hooky. When you're young, from school. When you're older, from life."

—Anonymous

You've always meant to go, haven't you? To the aquarium. To the museum. To the planetarium. To the zoo. You've promised yourself every time you've driven past the place: "One of these days . . ."

So make it *today,* and make a day of it. A leisurely, stroll-don't-run kind of day. No fair peeking at your watch or a clock. Whether it is just one or some or all of the places you've always meant to explore for the first time, or whether it is a repeat visit, GO. Don't wait. There will always be a reason why you can't. Create a reason why you must.

And when you get home and reflect, you'll think: *Gee, I didn't do much today, did I? Then again, I did. I did a lot, I saw a lot, I learned a lot. Best of all, I made good on a promise to myself . . .*

LET THE CHILD OUT

98

"Any child with sense knew you didn't involve yourself with the adult world if you weren't absolutely forced to."

—Jill Tweedie

"Childhood is the Last Chance Gulch for happiness. After that, you know too much."

—Tom Stoppard

They're still in there, you know. The little boy, the little girl you were once upon a time. They're still in there, believe it or not. Guess what? They are dying to come out and play, if only you'd let them.

So, go back. Go to a park. Go to a playground. Listen to the laughter and the squeals and the shouts.

Feel that pulling around your mouth? That's called a smile. If no one's looking—heck, even if they are—get in a swing and soar with the birds.

Go fly a kite. Blow some bubbles. Build a snowman. Toast some marshmallows. When you're done, you can put the child back. But whisper this promise: *We'll do it again. And soon.*

99

TAKE A PARENT TO LUNCH

"Funny, but the older I get the smarter my parents become."

—Anonymous

"There are times when parenthood seems nothing but feeding the mouth that bites you."

—Peter de Vries

Talked to Mom lately? When was the last time you saw your Pop? No, no, this isn't the start of a monster guilt trip. Just a thought: *How about inviting one or both to lunch?* Your treat.

You will, to paraphrase Dirty Harry, make their day. The meal won't really matter. Neither will who picks up the tab. It's the *gesture,* the thought, the consideration that counts. And above all, the hug. Both the one before and the one after. There might even be one during the meal. You never know.

You're going to feel better than you have in a long time.

Oh, and a couple more things: Sit up straight! Elbows off the table! Don't chew with your mouth open! And no dessert until you clean your plate! Any of that sound familiar?

SENSE THE SENSES 100

> "*Of all the senses the one considered to be the most useful is the sense to come in out of the rain.*"

—Anonymous

> "*Nothing can cure the soul but the senses, just as nothing can cure the senses but the soul.*"

—Oscar Wilde

We take them—all five of them—for granted. We're never really aware of them until, oh say, that change in altitude in a plane temporarily takes away our hearing. Or the sun blinds us momentarily. Or the heavy head cold makes all food taste like cardboard and an onion and a rose smell the same.

So take the time to enjoy your senses, and all of the sensations that they make possible. Don't just look, *observe*. There's a difference.

Inhale and savor the scent of roses and everything else.

Put down the salt and pepper, and permit your taste buds to work.

Enjoy the subtle and myriad colors of a rainbow.

Feel silk, feel burlap, feel satin, feel sandpaper.

Listen . . . to birds, to children, to the beating of your own heart.

101

TAKE
INVENTORY

"When you begin to count up your blessings, you're liable to run out of fingers. And toes."
—Adapted from Confucius

"A thankful heart is the parent of all virtues."
—Cicero

Periodically, stores will take stock of their stock. They say they're taking inventory. They check every shelf, every back room, every nook, every cranny. Then they write it down, total it up, and eventually arrive at an approximate reckoning of what they have on hand exactly.

I heartily recommend this process for all of us. Usually we get around to it once a year on Thanksgiving or New Year's Day. But don't wait. Start a list, in your mind or even on paper, of all in your life for which you are grateful.

Family, friends, and health, of course, but also your unique blessings.

Pretty soon, the rest—the material stuff, the daily grind—doesn't seem to matter so much. You might even wonder why you've been chasing after them so hard.

The best thing about a personal inventory is that it is a guaranteed blues buster. You always end up feeling overwhelmed for all that you do have, and what you thought you'd been wanting no longer seems all that important.

118

MAKE A
HOUSE CALL 102

"I enjoy convalescence. It is the part that makes illness worthwhile."
—George Bernard Shaw

"Behold, I do not give lectures or a little charity / When I give I give myself."
—Walt Whitman

While there are times when we all secretly like to wallow in our misery, being sick or hurt gets old in a hurry, especially if it is being done in solitude.

An unexpected phone call or visit can perk you up, especially if you're in a hospital, so return the favor. As with most things, when you give of your time and yourself, you're the one who'll feel better.

So bring sympathy and solicitude, some humor, and maybe a pen to sign a cast. Snacks are rarely rejected. Above all, come with a silent promise to yourself that you won't show them your scar or talk about your chronic illness. Your visit is about them.

103 HAPPY BIRTHDAY TO YOUUUUU . . .

"It's easier to get older than it is to get wiser."
—Anonymous

"The return of my birthday, if I remember it, fills me with thoughts which it seems to be the general care of humanity to escape."
—Samuel Johnson

Though some of us may pretend that it doesn't matter, or protest that we don't want a fuss made, deep down our birthday is special to each of us. In fact, the only thing that means more, if we're honest, is our own name.

So honor the birth date of the special people in your life.

There are a lot of ways to send birthday wishes now—by e-mail or snail mail, by card or by courier, by fax or by phone.

Or, best of all, in person.

Some will say age is just a number. Some will say they don't celebrate them anymore. But secretly, they'll be grateful and touched that you cared.

BOOK YOUR MOMENTS 104

"You can close your eyes to reality, but not to memories."
—Anonymous

"Quite literally, a man's memory is what he forgets with."
—Odell Shepard

Probably, they're scattered about your house or apartment. In a drawer. In a shoebox. Wedged between some books. At the bottom of that pile of magazines.

Scraps. Not leftover bits of food, but bits of history.

Photographs. A hair ribbon. The program from a graduation. A wedding matchbook. An anniversary napkin. They all have two things in common: They instantly trigger memories, and they all fit right into a scrapbook.

So round them up, glue them in, and you will have created your own book, one that no publisher can duplicate (although Running Press would try!).

105 BROWSE, SCAN, SAMPLE

"I read part of it all the way through."
—Samuel Goldwyn

"A good book contains more real wealth than a good bank."
—Roy L. Smith

Is there a more magical place anywhere than inside a bookstore? It is a buffet for the mind and the imagination. Shelves upon shelves of knowledge and entertainment are all there for your leisurely browsing.

Sample to your heart's content. There is no finer way to pass an hour (or three) than inching your way down the aisles, scanning titles, admiring book jackets, reading a page (or twenty!), and then moving on.

You suddenly discover an interest for Irish history. You giggle over a book of cartoons in the Humor section. You read staff recommendation cards and check out the new releases.

All those volumes remind you of how much you have to learn and experience—and where you can come to do just that.

"Life is like a box of chocolates . . ."
—Forrest Gump

"One does not discover new lands without consenting to lose sight of the shore for a very long time."
—André Gide

There's a smorgasbord waiting for you out there, just beyond your front door. A high school band concert. A Broadway play. A Little League game. A flower show. A new restaurant opening.

The choices are virtually limitless, and what you settle on isn't important. What does matter is that you sample it, that you feel the sun on your face and inhale a crisp winter night, that you get rained upon, that you kick at leaves.

Open up a local paper and check out your local offerings.

Open yourself to the efforts and wonders of others. Marvel at their talents. You'll get a new appreciation for the human condition.

107 TAKE "NO" FOR AN ANSWER
(but don't stop asking)

"Just because you say no doesn't mean I can't get you to change your mind."

—Salesman's creed

"Over-emphatic negatives always suggest that what is being denied may be what is really being asserted."

—Jonathan Raban

Here's the trick: Believe what your ears hear, just don't accept it. If you get a rejection, try to think of it as an improvement in the odds. The chances of "Yes" keep improving with each "No."

Providing, of course, that you keep on trying.

The best example of all: Dr. Theodore S. Geisel. He wrote a book. He went to a publishing house with his book and he heard: "No." He kept hearing "No" but he kept knocking on publishers' doors, and after hearing "No" a staggering twenty-three times, he finally heard "Yes."

You know him by his pen name: Dr. Seuss. His books have sold more than 200 million copies. He could have written the definitive one about persistence.

CHECK OUT THE OBITS 108

"The reports of my demise have been greatly exaggerated."
—Mark Twain

"No man should be afraid to die, who hath understood what it is to live."
—Thomas Fuller

Each newspaper contains a section of fascinating history. It is the obituary page, and on it are the condensed life stories of people who have recently passed on.

Read them and you will learn of triumph and tragedy, glory and misdeeds. You may be inspired and you certainly will be educated. There is something to be gleaned from every life, good example or bad.

And it's surprisingly life affirming. These people lived and loved. Their lives remind us that time is not to be squandered and every moment should be savored. Our number will be up soon enough; don't waste even one more minute waiting for it.

109 HAVE GREAT EXPECTATIONS

"Optimism is the belief that everything is beautiful, including what is ugly."

—Ambrose Bierce

"Man's real life is happy, chiefly because he is ever expecting that it soon will be so."

—Edgar Allan Poe

The pessimist says that things have a way of turning out pretty much like you expect them to turn out. Wonderful! Let's hope that's true.

Why? Because all you need to do is to turn that around. The strategy is to be expectant about what is to come, rather than cringing at its approach.

Expect only good things.

Try starting the day with a sense of anticipation. That doesn't mean you should be so wowed by the roses that you don't see the thorns. But it is possible to be both a realist and a dreamer.

Come to think of it, that's the ideal balance, isn't it?

GIVE A HUNDRED AND TEN PERCENT 110
(You were expecting another number?)

"Life is playing the violin in public and learning the instrument as you go along."
—Lord Bulwer-Lytton

"I love living. I have some problems with my life, but living is the best thing they've come up with so far."
—Neil Simon

Every coach and athlete has used the number 110 at one time or another. Theoretically, of course, it should not be possible. One hundred percent, mathematically, is the highest point.

But of course we're not talking theory or numbers, we're talking effort, spirit, attitude, enthusiasm, drive, determination, the willingness to push the envelope, all the things that define the fierce and unbending indomitability of the human spirit.

So, you can let life happen to you, or . . .

You can wrap your arms tightly around it and smile and ask: "May I have this dance?"

Let Pat Croce's success story inspire you to score big in life!

THE NEW YORK TIMES BESTSELLER

PAT CROCE
Author of *110%*

I Feel Great
and you will too!

AN INSPIRING JOURNEY OF SUCCESS
WITH PRACTICAL TIPS ON HOW
TO SCORE BIG IN LIFE

WITH BILL LYON

Foreword by Bill Cosby

0-7432-2213-X • $14.00

FIRESIDE
A Division of Simon & Schuster
A VIACOM COMPANY